AIRPORT STORIES

By

ASHA PONNACHAN

www.rhyvers.press   mail@rhyvers.com

Title: **AIRPORT STORIES**
Edition: **First-2024**

First published 2024 by Rhyvers Press
1515 Pataudi House, Darya Ganj, New Delhi, India

ISBN: 978-81-970083-1-3   MRP: 200/   Pages: 72

ALL RIGHTS RESERVED
No part of this book may be reproduced or transmitted in any form by any means, electronic or mechanical, including photocopy, recording or information storage and retrieval system, without permission in writing from the author (copyright owner) and publisher.

Language: **English**

This book is sold subject to the condition that it shall not, by way of trade or otherwise, be lent, resold, hired out, or otherwise circulated without the publisher's prior consent in any form of binding or cover other than that in which it is published and without a similar condition including this condition being imposed on the subsequent purchaser.

Typeset in Book Nimrod MT
Printed in India at Thomson Press (India) Limited
Email: rhyverspress@gmail.com Website: www.rhyvers.press

Dedication

This book is dedicated to my little darlings- Daniel and David

Acknowledgements

Where do I start? How can I end this section? I have been blessed to know and receive the love and support of so many people. Each person having taught me something that has influenced me as an artist, as a writer.
Perhaps I will start with those who have been part of my journey from the beginning- a huge thank you to my family. Through all my crazy, impractical and impulsive decisions, such as giving up a steady corporate job, you stood by me. I couldn't have pursued my passion without your support.
I would like to thank each friend who encouraged me. When things looked dim, you shone the light- some of you standing right next to me and some, from miles away. I am grateful each day for all of you.
My language teachers who instilled in me the love of words at an early age are a constant reminder of how noble and passionate educators can mould the minds and lives of people. I remember you and I thank you.
I am indebted to the readers who have read my words whether in the form of my books, online publications, social media posts or any other version.
Thank you Rhyvers Press for your faith in my work as an author!

FOREWORD:
It must feel rather strange to work at an airport

There you are, getting ready every morning, to get to work at a ticketing counter, a security check-point, a baggage handling area, even at an air traffic control tower. To see and to assist hundreds, verily thousands of passengers, every day, en route to their destinations, to places they need to go for business, to meet their loved ones, for Diwalis and Christmases and Eids and Hannukahs, for birthdays and for bereavements.

And to realize, that despite being at an airport that sees a countless airplanes departing and landing from the tarmac, there you are, grounded, at the same place, sans wings to fly.

And yet, even in those moments of odd epiphany, even in those transient timepods of perhaps being able to strike a relationship with travelers, eventually it comes down to being a witness to so many stories. Indeed, you do have a window seat when you work at an airport. Only, it's a window into the lives of passengers.

That is where Asha Ponnachan's 'Airport Stories' comes in. It turns the gaze away from the stories of passengers, and instead indirectly narrates them through the stories of people who work at an airport. An interesting construct that allows these short stories to hold a mirror to the best and worst in human character. A smorgasbord of human emotions – from hope to despair, cowardice and courage, love and letdowns.

Come, your ticket to enter the worlds of Ameena and Bipin, Sheila and Alam, Sylvie and Jayden, and many such personas, is ready. Board your flight, relax in your seat, fasten your safety belt, and turn the pages as you ascend into a cloud of colored tales.

Shantesh S Row
copywriter, scriptwriter and CCO who has inspired over 500 brands

Contents

1. A Gift for Abba 1
2. Varalakshmi travels abroad 13
3. The Travelling Professor 22
4. The Return 31
5. Yes, but… 41
6. An odd day… 55

"and the last of her treasured memories disappeared as the auctioneer's gavel thundered...sold to the lowest bidder."
- asha (hope)

A Gift for Abba

Shift change is always a crazy time with inventory counts and managers checking tills at each customer service station. The never-ending throng of passengers flowing like tributaries on a quest adds to the chaos. In spite of this being a daily occurrence, every changeover carried the same anxiety, as though some unimagined mishap would occur with irreparable consequences. Most days would go without the adventure of a mishap and even when one did occur, the consequences were not worthy of apprehension. Yet the cycle of neurotic chaos followed by loudly expressed relief would continue day after day. This was where Ayman worked; at the international airport and one of the finest airports at that.

It was a Friday evening, and she was scheduled for the night shift. Coming out of two consecutive evening shifts with her waking hours devoted to schoolwork for her distance learning program, Ayman was overworked and sleep deprived. Tonight, was not even her shift, she was covering for Aoife who had yet another family emergency. It was rather odd, how Aoife's family emergencies seemed to coincide with her boyfriend's arrival in town. "Oh well! I can use the extra pay", thought Ayman. Thus decided, her Friday night was going to be spent counting inventory, cleaning shelves, serving travellers who are 'just looking' and tendering change in the local currency.

Suppressing more than a few yawns, she waits for Kiko to tally the sales from her shift. "You are always tired these days. What's going on?", chimes Kiko as she tries to track down the missing 100 euros from her cash sales. Stifling yet another yawn, Ayman, mumbled something about schoolwork. Before she could complete her elucidation on the travails of obtaining an undergraduate degree while working full time, Vinay, duty manager for Friday's night shift walks up to them with a questioning glance. "Hello ladies", his words doused with creepy overtones and perverted undertones elicits nothing but eyerolls from the 'ladies'. As he passes them by with a warning that he will soon be back, Ayman, now on her guard against this danger of the night, whispered under her breath, "and he wonders why he is still single….ewwww…blech". Kiko was only too happy that her shift was nearly over and she would soon be transported home, miles away from Vinay. Her happiness was doubled at the sight of a 100 Euro note stuck to the side of the cash bag which she had already checked twice. "Well, third time's a charm!", said Kiko, "now let's go over the inventory and then I can go home to 'Netflix and chill', if you know what I mean". Kiko's current partner of not more than three weeks, like all her previous partners, was anything but a favourite with Ayman. "What is wrong with you? Seriously, what do you see in him?" asked Ayman. Kiko shooed her questions away with an elegant wave and a crude booty shake. She was like that-playful, regal, sensuous, crude, all at once.

Ray-Ban, Versace, Police, Michael Kors, Costa, Prada, Bulgari, Dior and all the rest of those wonderfully luxurious brands neatly checked off on the inventory sheet, both girls signed their names and stock count was completed. "Ding-dong", chimed the airport announcement system, "Attention all passengers. Any baggage left unattended will be removed from the terminal by security and may be destroyed. Please do not leave your baggage unattended", said a kindly yet unfeeling voice from the other side of ubiquitous speakers. "What a pity that does not extend to emotional baggage", exclaimed Kiko as she picked up her cash bag, till, sales notes and end-of-shift sales report, making her way to the back office. There an eager accountant sat with his fingers flying over the numerical keys of a keyboard. This was the sanctum of the duty-free shop, where only the chosen, the duty-free staff, were allowed to enter. Those who set foot into this inner chamber must bring with them a sacrifice of credit card receipts and banknotes. The more the better. When exiting, each member must be cleansed through a careful examination of pockets, purses and souls. Those found without blemish in action or intent would have completed the ritual and would be allowed to leave with the promise of their day's wages at an appointed time. Usually everyone who entered this inner domain, exited without cause for concern.

Meanwhile, in the outside world, subject to the curious eyes of occasional travellers and disinterested eyes of frequent flyers, Ayman and her colleagues were busy arranging and re-arranging merchandise. Most travellers buzz through the airport with heads tilted back, eyes fixed on information screens, passports, phones and jackets in one hand while the other one tows a carry bag or child or both. A lower ratio of passengers visit the duty-free shops and an even lesser number of them actually buy anything. Yet the duty-bound sales staff are obligated to appear as though they're interested in selling their wares to each passerby. The shop floor boasted of all kinds of goods, from branded sunglasses to mass produced wooden camels, from mini massagers to Bulgari watches, from Godiva gold boxes to overpriced socks and Jo Malone perfumes. High value stations were manned by two people while the more common ones hosted a single staff member at its undervalued helm.

Ayman was busy wiping an entire evening's worth of fingerprints from some rather expensive sunglasses. Vinay slowly made his way over to her section and with all the appeal of a cockroach flipped on its back, he said, "so I guess you'll be spending tonight with me huh?...haha...get it night shift..night...huh?" Ayman nearly threw up. "Vinay, if you were the last man on earth and there were a million women left, the human race would still perish" she retorted. He opened his lecherous mouth to say something but before he could get the words out, customers strode over to the leather goods section. Ayman greeted them with enthusiasm and evident relief.

Standing in front of her was a woman clad in black coloured burqa complete with a niqab. Peering out of the black niqab were the loveliest pair of brown eyes that Ayman had seen. They were warm and maternal with the faint memory of stolen youth. The bordering soft black cloth seemed to emphasize something deep in those eyes- questions burdened with requests, meekness mixed with mild defiance. Ayman's customary greeting was lost in her admiration of the woman when a rough noise broke this gentle scene with its untimely ingress. The noise seemed to emanate from a nearly-sixty-year-old man with an unpleasant demeanour standing two feet away from our woman and her beautiful brown eyes. He possessed, by contrast, a pair of wide-set rheumy eyes barely supported by eyelids that were permanently scrunched. Their angry gaze matched the rest of his ill-mannered self. A heavy mixture of disagreeable odours surrounded his lank frame replacing substance with stench. He approached the burqa clad woman with a familiarity that disconcerted Ayman. "How can this delicate woman possibly be related to someone like him?", she thought. At the expense of a few words, it was established that they were not only related but intimately so; they were husband and wife. For the second time that night, Ayman nearly threw up.

The woman spoke softly in short spurts as though afraid that her voice would betray her and it did. She sounded far too young to be married, let alone be the wife of the displeasing creature standing next to her wearing a threatening scowl and an overpowering body odour. He was hurrying her on with animated gestures while she quietly browsed the items on display. Every time she pointed to a product, his hands would pull up the price tag and there would be a loud exclamation signifying 'no' rather dramatically. The woman shot occasional glances at Ayman who stood watching this entire production unfold in disbelief and confusion. Just then the airport speakers chimed, breaking the fourth wall and Ayman was stirred to action. She decided to enter the ongoing production. It was clear that the woman spoke no English, so Ayman asked for her boarding pass by pointing to the piece of paper sticking out of her handbag. She immediately handed it over. This interaction roused the husband's suspicion, and he came dangerously close to them. Ayman held her breath. Ignoring her extreme discomfort at not only the invasion of her personal space but also the assault on her olfactory sense, Ayman braved the situation. The name on the boarding pass read 'Rahman, A. Bushra'. The destination was Hyderabad, India and boarding was not for another two hours.

"Bushra", said Ayman gently. The woman looked up, her doe like eyes overcome with emotion. A single tear clung bravely to her lashes. They shared a moment so wrought with sentiment that even the husband fell silent, briefly loosening his scowl. Alas, the moment did not last. His brusque manner returned all too soon and with it a volley of words intended to rush his wife.

Bushra flinched a little but did not hurry her actions. Whether it was the tenderness in Ayman's voice or the safety offered by the airport's public space, something rendered a change in Bushra's attitude albeit a slight one. She was not going to be hurried. Once again, perusal of the items on display began. This time with more careful consideration much to her husband's chagrin. Noting the long wait till their flight's boarding time, Ayman returned Bushra's boarding pass. Taking a clue from their destination, she decided to speak in Urdu. She opened with a compliment and Bushra taken aback at first, quickly realized the offer of friendship with a grateful response. Their conversation did not run smoothly though, as Bushra's ever vigilant husband was constantly hovering about with a menacing glare. Every now and then he would yell something at Bushra in a dialect of Arabic that Ayman did not understand.

Bushra wanted to look at a belt that was placed low on the shelf. As she tried to bend, she placed a hand on her belly, which had its own tale to tell, for support. Ayman quickly picked up the belt and showed it to her, voicing words of congratulations at the same time. Bushra forced a smile and said 'shukriya' but there was a catch in her throat, a lowering of her eyes and a deep sigh. Ayman read between words that were not uttered. Here was a teen bride, forced to accept a life thrust upon her with never a say in it. At the end of her sigh she said, "humaari qismat aur kya" (it's just my fate) in a resigned voice. Ayman, handing her the belt she had picked touched her gently on the arm. This act of empathy seemed to overcome any last reservations that Bushra held, and words formed full sentences pouring forth her story.

She was the first born of seven children: six girls and one boy. Her family possessed meagre resources and life was hard. Often Bushra and her mother would subsist on one meal a day so that the others had enough to eat. Her parents dreamed of sending their son to a good school so he could become a doctor, a dream that was well beyond their exiguous means.

One afternoon, a relative showed up unannounced at their door. Uncle Bashir worked in the middle east and visited annually for his month-long vacation. This time, he had 'good news' for Bushra's mother. He brought news of a 'rishta' (wedding alliance) for Bushra and with it a solution to all their penurious problems. 'Mr. Rahman', he intimated, 'was a well to do man and would give a large sum as mehar (dowry) to the bride or bride's family'. Amma smiled with relief for the first time in years and offered him more tea. Abba looked suspicious. Upon learning that Mr. Rahman was nearly as old as himself, Abba said the whole idea was preposterous and refused to entertain the conversation any further. Amma, however, had six other children and their futures to consider. She invited uncle Bashir to stay for dinner and together they worked on persuading Abba. While they conceded that Mr. Rahman was much older than Bushra, they contended that he could give her a 'good life'. She would go abroad. Amma reminded Abba that he could never manage to send any of his children abroad, no matter how much milk he sold! The final straw was the possibility of sending chotu to a reputable school. Before dinner was done, there were talks of moving to the city. Using the mehar money, they could buy a house close to the medical college where chotu would eventually study. Chotu was six years old when he sat down to dinner that evening and by nightfall everyone had started calling him doctor saab. Amma talked incessantly about a brighter future for everyone, and the children heartily ate the chocolates that Uncle Bashir had brought them from 'abroad'. Thus, on that night, amidst the relief of her parents and merriment of her siblings, Bushra's fate was decided for her; to be a dutiful daughter, a dutiful wife and a good mother.

Uncle Bashir made all the arrangements, and, in a month, young Bushra became a married woman. She met her groom for the first time on their wedding day and immediately discarded any lingering hopes of happiness for herself. She was, however, happy for her family and held on to that thought through out the ceremony maintaining the semblance of smile. Mr. Rahman, true to his word, provided a generous mehar, or at least it was generous when converted to rupees. The wedding festivities lasted for 2 days, after which Bushra left the country with her husband to her new home. She said goodbye to the rest of her family at home but Abba came to the airport to see her off. Before entering the airport, Bushra hugged her father one last time and as she turned to leave, Abba whispered, "mujhe maaf kardena beta" (please forgive me my child). They stood for a moment in silence, each understanding the plight and helplessness of the other. That was the first time her husband had interrupted an emotional moment in his coarse manner. She let go of her father's hand and donned the new role of a dutiful wife. That was two years ago. She had not seen her family for these two long years and during the rare phone calls she was allowed, it was Amma who spoke to her.

Last week, she received news that her father was unwell, and things were looking dire. Mr. Rahman finally consented to take her to Hyderabad but not without constantly impressing upon her the great pecuniary strain it caused him. That, explained Bushra, is why he was in such a foul mood. Ayman disregarded her last statement suspecting that Mr. Rahman knew no other moods.

Bushra looked at the belt in her hand feeling the material tenderly as though memories of her childhood were embedded on it. Amma had not provided details of Abba's condition, but Bushra knew in her heart that he didn't have long to live.

As children, she and her siblings rarely received any gifts. However, every year, on the day of the annual village fair, Abba would bring home a gift for each one of them. The year before Bushra's wedding, he had just enough money to buy a small bag of lemon flavoured hard candy which they shared. Abba always said, "tohfa kitna bhi chota ho, dil bada hona chahiye" (no matter how small the gift is, it's the giver's large heart that matters). Now, going to visit Abba for what would most likely be the last time, she wanted to buy him a small gift; one that her meagre allowance and Rahman's miserly heart would allow. It was this endeavour that brought her to Ayman's counter at the duty-free shop. Even though she knew that he probably wouldn't be able to use it, Bushra wanted desperately to take home a gift for Abba.

Lost in her story, Ayman had all but forgotten about Rahman until his gnarled hand came up and snatched the belt from Bushra. Once again, looking at the price tag, he huffed and puffed waving his hands in the air. Bushra stood defeated. The single tear that clung to her lashes earlier, now slid down bringing with it a steady stream of more tears. This scene attracted the attention of people passing by and soon a crowd gathered at the wearables counter. The crowd drew the attention of other duty-free staff, security guards and the floor manager. Rahman found himself surrounded by strangers, all of whom were clearly judging him. One of the guards came over and asked if there was an issue. Before Ayman could explain, Rahman grabbed his purse from the pocket of his thobe and pulled out some cash. His eyes betraying fear, embarrassment and anger, he barked at Ayman to take the payment and give him the bill. She completed the transaction quickly, placed the belt in a lovely little gift box and handed it to a surprised Bushra.

Rahman, visibly outraged by this entire episode, grabbed the bill from Ayman, then turned and walked away trying to avoid the crowd. Bushra, clutching her treasure, followed slowly behind her husband. The airport speakers chimed with some urgent last call for passengers flying to Copenhagen, the crowd dispersed, Vinay came running to Ayman's counter and the shift returned to its normal drill. A few minutes later, a new stream of travellers flooded the airport bringing with them new stories to be told, relegating Bushra and her gift to a distant memory.

"words like embroidered threads weave in and out of thoughts, sewing my lips and not a sound is heard."

-asha (hope)

Varalakshmi travels abroad

Rambling in a foreign language, her words stumbled one upon the other. The ageing lines etched on her young face communicated well, a story of desperation, a story of hope. She found both but in which order and at what cost.

As one staff member paged for a translator, another tried to comfort her and yet another continued explaining laws regarding visas and entry into the country. Her light brown eyes brimming with tears darted uncomprehendingly from one person to the other. All three of these airport employees found their efforts unsuccessful. While the staff on duty spoke a variety of languages, none could understand this frail passenger who held all her worldly possessions in a tightly wrapped bundle of cloth.

A rather rotund security guard descended upon the pitiful scene crudely proclaiming his authority to deal with matters such as "illegal entry". Whether it was the guard's ill-fitting uniform threatening to burst at the seams, his garrulous nature or his uncompromising volume that proved to be the last straw, is uncertain. Perhaps it was their insensitive combination that bore upon the poor woman's depleting strength as her tears streamed down accompanied by silent sobs. This seemed to unnerve the security guard and his voluble pronouncements dissolved into a confused mumble.

The air-conditioned airport presented a frigid wall to Varalakshmi's entreaties. She stood at the counter shivering partly from fear and partly from the cold. Wrapped in a worn-out cotton saree mismatched with a tattered blouse, her attire provided little to no protection against the elements, climatic or otherwise. Her appearance so forlorn clashed with the bright lights and festive décor all around. It was the season to be jolly and she was anything but jolly.

As Eartha Kitt crooned her requests to Santa Baby through pervasive speakers, passengers from multiple flights flooded the airport's duty-free shops, lounges, eateries, immigration lines, baggage collection, washrooms and every other area possible. Parents with children in tow, travel guides with tourists in tow, general populace with overstuffed carry-ons in tow and those travelling for business with little more than loud, apathetic conversations to show. The seasonal spangle provided ample opportunities for social media aficionados to photograph their way through the airport, documenting every inch of their journey. There was a general atmosphere of cheer everywhere; well... everywhere except at one security counter.

After much searching of records, it was discovered that one of the duty-free staff came from the same town as shown on Varalakshmi's passport. Finally, a breakthrough!

Aanya, a wholesome, bright eyed, curly haired custodian of never-ending cheerfulness was at home enjoying her day off when she received the phone call. An immigration officer and the duty manager working that shift summoned her to the airport providing as little information as possible. Aanya, wolfing down the last slice of pizza quickly donned her freshly laundered uniform and rushed to the chartered airport taxi waiting outside. Aadil, the driver, was a well known and well-loved face among his colleagues. It was rumoured that there might have been a little too much knowing and even more loving going on between Aadil and some of his female colleagues. Rumours are as rumours go and irrespective of their veracity or lack thereof, he was a friendly person whose company Aanya enjoyed. They had not shared a shift for many weeks so there was quite a lot to catch up- tv shows, new restaurants and workplace gossip. "Speaking of work, there's quite the drama unfolding at the airport tonight", said Aadil. "Well, that's why they sent for the specialist", joked Aanya. He produced an obligatory smile to his friend's quip and proceeded to explain the situation. The explanation however, produced more confusion than the message she received from her manager which was ambigious in itself. She wondered out loud, "why would they call in a duty-free staff member to resolve an immigration related matter? None of this makes any sense." As they pulled into the designated parking lot, Aadil replied, "well you will soon find out. Keep me posted, won't you?" She nodded in the affirmative and got out of the car. As Aanya turned to leave, he couldn't resist a little flirting, suggestively providing various options to spend the rest of the evening after she was done 'saving the day'. She rolled her eyes in mock displeasure and mumbled a rather certain "maybe" before rushing inside.

She was met at the arrivals section by Mr. Abdul, a highly placed immigration officer who carried his responsibilities with the appropriate mixture of gravity and humility, a rare and appealing quality. "Sorry to drag you in to work today but we have a bit of a situation here and I am told you can help", said Mr. Abdul. "Well, I am happy to do so, except I am still rather unclear about what is going on. The messages I have received till now have been…a bit cryptic", replied Aanya. He quickly laid the case before her, "The facts as we know them are few. Mrs. Varalakshmi is in possession of a fake visa and cannot be allowed to enter the country. At the moment, her arrival here is illegal. However, we haven't been able to gather any further information from her and that is where you come in. We are hoping you can speak to her in a language she understands." Aanya nodded while striving to keep pace with Mr. Abdul who whizzed them through all the checkpoints with his high security clearance pass. Nearly breathless, she reached the windowless room where Varalakshmi was seated with a small cup of lukewarm tea and the large form of a dour guard.

Mr. Abdul pulled up a couple of chairs and made the mandatory introductions.

Aanya, forsaking English, reintroduced herself in her language to Varalakshmi whose silence broke with alacrity. She poured forth entire volumes in a stream of sentences and tears. Only, this time, the tears were those of relief. The lukewarm tea was exchanged for a hot meal of rice, dal and potato sabzi. The frosty airport room started to acquire some semblance of warmth. Hours of silence was replaced with untamed emotional conversation. When they offered her pepsi to drink, she hesitated ever so slightly before taking the can and cradling it in her hands. This fizzy delight titillated Varalakshmi's inexperienced palette and she appeared to savour every drop with a sense of guilty pleasure. For a brief moment in time, her worries seemed to disappear, and her weary face relaxed a little. There appeared a smile on her face and the years fell away in a matter of minutes. Aanya sat wondering at the transformation. The haggard woman she was speaking with, only minutes earlier, was now a young woman in her late twenties albeit with twenty years of hard labour behind her.

She explained to Aanya that the landlord in her village would buy cans of pepsi for his children whenever he went to the city. Varalakshmi's husband rented the farm from him, and they worked hard. Even her sons helped with farm work after school. However, over the past few years, their crops seemed to fail season after season thrusting them further into debt. It was a hot summer's day when for the fifth month in a row last year, she went to ask the landlord for an extension on the rent they owed him. Her sons went with her, and they were parched by the time they reached his house.

The landlord had returned from the city that morning with his usual bounty of soft drinks. His children were sitting on the porch fighting the scorching heat with Pepsi, sometimes sipping the drink and sometimes holding semi-cold cans to their perspiring foreheads. While she entreated the landlord who seemed to be running out of patience, her sons looked on with longing at those precious, unattainable cans of sugary thirst quenchers. The landlord offered them neither a drink nor an extension for rent payment and they walked home despondent, each mile exacting thirst and extracting hope from their fragile bodies. She despaired of breaking the news to her husband. Incessant hard labour, compounding debt and constant worry had been taking a toll on his health. However, upon reaching home, she found her husband smiling and chatting with a guest. She hadn't seen him smile in months! He introduced the guest as Balan, his nephew's friend from the city.

Balan had started his own business in the city after graduating from college. He offered jobs and visas for people to go 'abroad', an opportunity to leave a life of penury and build a good life, a golden opportunity as he put it. Oh! the dreams he wove for them that night sitting on their kutcha veranda. All their worries seemed to fade away in the steam rising from his glass of black tea. That night they found hope. Little did they know that it would disappear like the smoke rising from the end of his cheap cigarette.

Before Balan left that night, it was decided that he would find 'aunty' Varalakshmi, a job in the middle east. He would take care of everything including the visa and since they are his friend's relatives, he offered to forego his usual service fees. Instead, they would only have to pay for the visa and air ticket which he would arrange through an affordable payment scheme. It wasn't until Varalakshmi disembarked the flight and was accosted at the arrivals by immigration officers that she began to understand Balan's scheme.

In their desperation to get out of debt, Varalakshmi and her husband grasped at the chance of her going 'abroad' to earn some much-needed money. Two weeks later, Balan sent them news that he had procured Varalakshmi a job as house help in the Middle East. Everything was an excited flurry of activities after that. For the first time since her wedding, Varalakshmi had photos taken and for the first time ever, she had a passport made. They borrowed more to pay for her visa and travel. Even though the interest rate was exorbitant, they didn't have much of a choice. This job seemed nothing short of a miracle, the answer to all their problems. Approximately two months after Balan's visit, Varalakshmi boarded a plane making for another first-time moment. This was a season of many firsts for her. She stopped talking at this point and stared at the Pepsi can in her hand, yet another first.

It was Aanya's turn now to fill in the details on why she was being detained. Although, by this time, Varalakshmi had begun to suspect some foul play with the visa, she did not know exactly what was wrong or the potential consequences for her. Shocked at the cruel trajectory life had drawn for this woman, Aanya found herself at a loss for words. "How could so many things go wrong in one person's life? How will she react to the fact that she can't even enter the country, let alone work here? What about the creditors? She can't stay here, she can't go back home- what will this poor woman do?", Aanya's mind was a whirlpool of hopeless thoughts. After much prompting from Mr. Abdul, she managed to fumble through a meagre explanation of Varalakshmi's visa being fake and possible deportation. They got no reaction from Varalakshmi who sat there, her face devoid of expression and her thoughts impassable. She sat still, exhausted from her long journey, from stress, from life.

After a few minutes, Mr. Abdul broke the awkward silence by thanking Aanya for coming in and talking to 'the passenger' as he called Varalakshmi. Now that the situation had been investigated, no fines or charges would be imposed, however, she would be deported with immediate effect. The injustice of Varalakshmi's circumstances plagued Aanya who found herself rooted to the floor, unable to walk out the door. She entreated Mr. Abdul to help her fellow citizen, her eyes now expressing the grief that Varalakshmi could no longer carry. After a few minutes of trying to extricate himself from this position with excuses about the situation being out of his hands, Mr. Abdul, agreed to talk to the chief immigration officer. There was, perhaps, hope after all. Translating the possibility of that hope for Varalakshmi to understand, Aanya left her there with a prayer and another can of Pepsi while she returned to spend the rest of her day off in silent contemplation.

*"and all these words lay around, wanting to be
picked up, held, understood, valued...
Yet for fear of being misunderstood,
they stay silent, hidden and subdued."*

- asha (hope)

The Travelling Professor

She made an effort today. After days of moping about trying to figure out that intricate string of curiosities called life, she threw her hands up in the air and decided it was time to try and enjoy it instead. So, she made an effort to dress up, to show up and generally move onward and upward with a smile, making the most of the day.

The airport information counter, however, had no spirit of mirth hovering over it and was not in the least bit accommodating of her pleasant efforts. As life would have it, her shift was changed to cover for a gap in the roster and she worked the information counter today. Passengers requiring information while not uncommon, the fact that so many of them were irate and less than civil in alarming synchronicity was rare. Perhaps this was a test of her perseverance thought Sylvie, a test that was teetering on turning her precarious smile upside down. There was the young mother travelling with her young child, toddler and visibly pregnant belly. She was tired, her child wanted an overrated and highly advertised toy from the duty-free shop and her toddler was being a toddler who was in the middle of a 21-hour flight. Nothing short of a miracle was going to make travel easier for this mom of 2 and a half children and no matter how pleasant Sylvie resolved to be, she was going to be one miracle too short. Mom wanted directions to the 'Parent's Rooms' and 'Activity Centres'. Upon learning that these sections were at least three travelators away in the direction she came from, it seemed likely that her toddler wouldn't be the only one throwing a tantrum. Thankfully, the irritation was confined to being uncivil in her reply and storming away belly first with child and toddler in tow. Then came the "first-class" ticket holder who found every lounge but the one he wanted. After waving his phone in Sylvie's face ensuring that she saw his "first-class" ticket, he made a few more comments about his being a frequent flyer, globetrotter and some bejewelled card holder or other, thereby making him deserving of better guidance than what he had received so far. His sense of entitlement clashed awkwardly with his desperate need to make Sylvie believe that he was indeed travelling 'first-class'. She in turn smiled and focused all her energy on keeping her ocular muscles from rolling her eyes. After eight months of working at the airport, she had mastered the art of disguising her disgust and delivering diplomatic dialogue while the devil danced on her tongue. Having sent him off to the desired lounge and dealt with one annoyed passenger after another with mechanical politeness and restraint worthy of sainthood, Sylvie closed her eyes and sighed. "Oh, please let the rest of the shift be peaceful or miraculously short or maybe both", prayed her inner voice.

No sooner than her thoughts reached their silent articulation, someone crooned a "good evening" in a deep voice with an accent usually reserved for the male protagonist of romantic novels. Her eyes opened to meet a pair of deep hazel ones set in a broad face which was at once rugged and soft, travel worn yet intense carrying an air of pride curiously mixed with gentle patience. Defying the need to blink she stared into his eyes acutely aware of them staring back at her with an equal defiance to blink. Suddenly, his stubble lined and slightly chapped lips curved into a smirk accompanying one of his unruly eyebrows that lifted in an amused guise. His faced flirted with a questioning glance. Her face answered with a rather perceivable blush and she swiftly lowered her gaze. Every minute seemed lengthened, and every heart beat rapid in complete contradiction to her prayer just a few moments ago but she couldn't have been more thankful. Her gratitude showed on her well moisturized glowing lips in the slightest hint of a smile. There was a curious glow in the air and the noise of the airport dimmed around her. Everything seemed to slow down, everything except her heart which was thumping so loudly, she was momentarily distracted from the hypnotic glance of her accoster who was still waiting for a reply. "Uh..um..good...good evening", said Sylvie her voice faltering and then quickly added, "may...may I help you?". "I sure hope so" rejoined the owner of the husky voice in a tone that mixed youthful mischief with unabashed immodesty. She lowered her eyes once more, her eyelids batting involuntarily. There was a warmth around her temples, rising in her cheeks, her neck and many other parts of her body which she did not wish to acknowledge, not in public, not while at work anyways. "Perhaps later", she thought, "when she got home, when she.." but his voice cut in before her thoughts were fully undressed. "My name is Jayden and my connecting flight has been delayed for 8 hours. I would like to use my time to explore a few tourist sites since they have given me a temporary entry visa. I was wondering if you could suggest some places to visit." Mr. Jayden provided this information in so matter-of-fact a manner that all the warmth drained from Sylvie's cheeks, neck, temples and everywhere else. She was rudely brought back to the present, awash with bright lights, loud announcements, and an interminable buzz of activity all around her. A heavy pang of inexplicable disappointment settled around her and replaced the earlier glow. Reigning in her maudlin emotions, she called on her inner professional and presented Jayden with a couple of brochures. "These list some of the more popular tourist attractions", she said with rather affected professionalism. He took the brochures from her and their fingers touched ever so briefly. All the earlier warmth returned in all the same places surging through her body, only this time it was hotter. She felt like she was on fire. She withdrew her trembling hands and did not know what to do with the rest of her trembling self, so she sat down on the tall stool behind the counter. He smiled, she melted. "Your colleague over there looked like he was a little too entertained by our conversation and I didn't want to get you into trouble but he seems to have lost interest now", said Jayden apologetically, placing the brochures back on the counter. "Oh so your flight is not delayed?" asked Sylvie with far more enthusiasm than she had intended to display. "What do you think?" Jayden teased. "I don't know what to think" she replied coyly. Not missing a beat, he suggested, "why don't we figure it out together over a cup of coffee?". "Well, my break isn't for another hour" said Sylvie sincerely hoping that wasn't going to be a problem. "Well, I'm not going anywhere", he joked. She laughed. "Now that's better", he said, "It simply didn't do to see you looking so glum". Taken aback she asked, "When was that?". "I saw those people before me give you a hard time and you looked like you were trying so hard. It can't be easy to do your job when people are mean. I just had to try and put a smile on your face", he explained. "Is that why you came over?" she enquired. This time, he answered with a smile that ended in neat little dimples on both cheeks. She nearly reached out and touched them. He interrupted her thoughts once again with a quick message that he'd be waiting for her upstairs at Costa Coffee and strode away with an unhurried gait as if he really had nowhere to go. "Ahem!" squeaked a short, stout woman who was weighing heavily on the arm of a tall, unhappy looking man who in turn bore the burden of repeating his wife's words. "Ahem" said the man. After which, squeak after squeak emanated from the woman about their luggage. Sylvie called the luggage office and the woman, her squeaks and her husband were all safely transported there. That problem solved, the remaining 45 minutes to her break passed very slowly but uneventfully. As soon as someone arrived to cover her break, she sprinted upstairs with all the grace of a springtime lamb but she didn't care.

He stood up as she reached their table, walked around to her side and standing close behind, pulled out a chair for her. She felt her knees buckle and gratefully slid into the chair. She was sure that she would all but dissolve if he came any closer. "I'll be right back", he whispered before going to collect their coffees and croissants.

"Chocolate croissants", she exclaimed her big brown eyes wide with amusement. "I love them". "I had hoped as much", replied Jayden wistfully. "Oh?" questioned Sylvie. "Well, here I am prattling on about me and I don't even know your name", returning to his playful tone. Confused, Sylvie hesitated for a moment unsure whether to press him about the croissants or to introduce herself. She settled for the latter. He did not respond and they sipped their coffees in silence. After a few minutes, Sylvie asked, "So where are you headed?". "Oh, wherever the wind takes me", he was flirting again. "Ok, what do you do?", she was determined to learn something about this enigmatic man. She liked a little mystery as much as the next girl but his evasiveness around his travel appeared slightly more concerning than mysterious. "I'm a professor", he offered promptly and that drove out any sprouting concerns in her mind. "Ah, what do you teach?" she continued. "Oh well, you know we all learn a lot more than we teach, don't we?", his evasiveness returned and so did her concerns. "Jayden, where exactly is the wind taking you?" she asserted her query. "She had the same hairstyle, you know". Sylvie was taken aback, "huh? Who? What are you talk..". "She loved chocolate croissants with black coffee. Sorry I didn't ask you how you like your coffee. Do you like it black?

A little too late to ask now, I guess..huh?" he carried on a confessional monologue.

This is where most people would have been worried enough to leave but Sylvie wasn't like most people. In fact, she had rarely met anyone with as much curiosity and resilience as she possessed.

Mentally shooing away a well meaning sense of apprehension, she said, "Oh that's just how I like my coffee…but..". "Ah, I thought as much", he said interrupting her mid-sentence. "She loved to travel. The destination didn't even matter as much to her. I think it was the idea of travelling that she loved so much. Airports, planes, ships, packing, unpacking, hotels, new places, people, culture everything. She really knew how to carpe her diem", and he laughed a happy laugh. Something didn't add up though. His words were happy, his lips were smiling but his eyes, they were lost, in a place far away where the mirth of his words couldn't reach. For all her curiosity she could not bring herself to pry into his sudden silence. An alarm rang on her phone signalling the end of her break. Their eyes met one last time and he spoke, slowly, dispassionately, "I wonder where the wind took her". Feeling uneasy for herself and a little embarrassed for him, she looked down at the coffee and croissants, now cold and as unappealing as he had become to Sylvie. Grabbing her phone and her purse, she murmured something about having to get back to work. As she was walking away, his voice floated above the din in the café, "Your smile is just like hers". Sylvie ran out of the café bumping into a colleague on the way. "Oh…Ameena…am I ever glad to see you", she muttered in a nervous attempt at small talk. Ameena, blissfully ignorant of the worried look on Sylvie's face, asked, "How does my hair look?". Before Sylvie could respond, Ameena waved to someone and entered the café, her words trailing behind her, "gotta run..have a date...talk to you later."

"in a world where life is fickle and death is faithful, keep your imaginations wild and your expectations tame..."

- asha (hope)

The Return

She hated working Wednesday evenings. Not only was it one of the busiest evenings of the week but it came with the added lack of attraction called Bipin, an odious excuse of a male biped parading as the duty manager. "Hello Amy", he drooled from the other side of the till distracting her from tallying the sales. "My name is AMEENA! If you must annoy me, at least call me by my name", she exclaimed, exasperated with his incessant attempts at hypocorism. "Oh ok Ms. Ameena", he retorted in mock obedience, "guess who gets to work my shifts again next week". He laughed, relishing the look of disgust on her face. Having sufficiently ruined her evening, he walked away to find another victim. She stood motionless watching his ungainly gait retreating into the office, wishing a hundred disasters upon him in succession.

"What did that toad want this time?". His voice startled Ameena. She turned to face the friendly voice and saw Faisal, her new colleague. Faisal had shadowed her for a couple of shifts during his first month at work. Now, three months in, he is already being slated for potential supervisory roles. She wasn't sure how she felt about it. Yes, he is qualified for the job but so is she. Yes, he shows initiative, but so does she and SHE had been showing initiative for almost a whole year. She had overheard one of the managers say that Faisal has a calm disposition. "Yeah, well he doesn't have to put up with the slimy attacks of specious creatures like Bipin. If he did, that would be the end of his CALM disposition..hmph!", she thought. This was quickly followed by other thoughts, "but he is always calm and helpful. Also, he always stands up for me and the rest of the team in his own unruffled way. I have to admire that. I hate that.He did peg Bipin as a toad. I like that. He will most likely get promoted before I do. I hate that. I think I like him but I am sure I don't like him."

"You might need those credit card receipts." Once again, Faisal's friendly voice made its way towards her and she was keenly aware of her tense disposition. "Huh?", she said confused and then looking down at her hands that were tightly clenched around the little pieces of paper from her sales register, she spoke again, "Oh!...Ohh! that ...that ...toad gets under my skin. Now I have to start all over again and I was almost done counting..ugh!!". "You know, the more annoyed you get, the more power he has over you", came Faisal's sagely advice. "Oh, don't you start now!!! If you have nothing more practical to say, then leave me and let me get on with my work. Your zen thing doesn't work for everyone", she spoke with misdirected anger. Immediately regretting her behaviour and knowing she could do with all the allies she could manage, she apologized, "I'm sorry. I …I am angry with him and well…it all sort of just ….sorry". Faisal stood by, waiting for her assortment of emotions to be expressed as they may. "Deep breaths do help and that's practical", he summed up their conversation with a smile and walked back to his station at the customer service counter. Ameena restarted tallying her sales for the evening, deep inhales and gracious exhales interspersing the cash count.

"Does that help?" piped a girlish voice from behind making Ameena jump and messing up her calculations. "Jen! What do you mean by sneaking up on me like that? Now I have to do this part again and that's the second time this evening." Jen's apologetic voice offered assistance with the process. Ameena, her deep breathing forgotten, and visibly ruffled said, "You might as well. You'll have to take over for your shift soon. The quicker we get this done, the better for the both of us. Oh! I hate this shift." Jen, in a further attempt to appease her work friend (for they were definitely not friends outside of work), offered, "Well at least it's over." Her wise words were met with a disgruntled grunt from Ameena whose surly mood seemed beyond salvation for the day. She had a sinking sensation all day, a foreboding about this day and even though it was almost over, she could not shake off the feeling. "I'm just being silly", she thought. "Or maybe it's this job. I should take a few days off and reconsider the…", her thoughts were interrupted by an audible gasp or atleast as audible as Jen's tiny person could afford. Ameena, determined to complete her shift's handover, ignored the sounds of surprise emanating from her colleague and continued with her end-of-shift paperwork. It wasn't until there came a collective gasp from the tide of human beings who had momentarily stopped their ebb and flow that Ameena lifted her head. People amassed in the centre of the transit area like iron filings on a magnet. Confusion hung in the air. Whispers turned into mutterings which turned into a buzzing chatter of voices all around. Jen stood rooted to the ground while Ameena ran towards the burgeoning crowd. All eyes were riveted on one man standing behind the glass banister on the top floor. The path to the departure gates were dotted with large ornate pots that held manicured fan palms, their leaves spread in finely arranged fans, each plant living up to its name. He stood there, looking tall in his khaki coloured kurta-pyjama. Suddenly, he looked taller still as he stepped on the rim of an ornate plant holder and that is all she would ever recall from the incident.

The airport rang with announcements, security personnel, ground staff, medical team and a host of other people running to the scene. Perhaps they were already there when she joined the crowd. Ameena couldn't be sure of the chronology of events. Had she heard the announcements before she saw him? Had he been there the whole time she was processing the end-of-shift report? Who was he? What just happened? She felt herself being pushed one way and another as the crowd dispersed. An arm grabbed her away from the melee and she found herself once again in the calm presence of Faisal. "Are you ok? Here, sit down", he said as he led Ameena back to her counter. Everything happened so quickly, she could scarcely process it. She felt shocked but was unable to understand the reason. "The man...did you see that man?" whispered a weak voice behind her. Ameena turned to find Jen seated on the floor, exhausted. She sat down next to her, equally exhausted. "I'm not sure, did you...see him?" croaked Ameena, her throat parched and beads of sweat on her forehead. Jen sighed in answer. Faisal brought them both water to drink. Other airport staff were milling about, everyone discussing 'the man'. That evening's shift was called to a quick close and announcements about 'an incident' boomed through the speakers. The rest of the evening was a blur. Faisal offered Ameena a ride home which she gratefully accepted. She did not want to share the ride home in the staff bus with people discussing 'the man' for another hour. She couldn't take another minute of it. She wanted some peace and quiet. She needed time to process the day, the evening, the incident and time was what she got.

Early Thursday morning, memos were sent to staff who worked the previous day's evening shift stating that they could avail themselves of two paid sick days in light of what the management described as "a distressing event". While she was still unsure of the actual event, Ameena knew she was distressed and rightfully availed the day off. She tried to distract herself with chores, errands, sleep, meditation, sufi music, fries, chips and ginger ale but nothing helped. "Who was he? What's his name? More importantly, how is he...is he still..?" Ameena's thoughts ran marathons in her head with no finish line in sight. As grim images passed through the kaleidoscope of her mind, her phone sounded indicating the arrival of a text message. "Hi, have you heard the latest?" It was Jen. Ameena's thoughts were provided with the relief of action. Jen, sweet, little Jen, had found out something. It took a few minutes before the command of the action filtered through the waves of Ameena's frenzied thoughts and reached her hands. Usually averse to phone calls, this 'texts only please' phone user, broke her own code and called Jen. This was important. This was urgent. A surprised Jen answered the call, "uh..hello?". Ditching the inconvenience of small talk, they dove into the heart of the matter. Jen had heard from Faisal, who had all the right friends in all the right places, that 'the man' had been the victim of forced labour. He had been in the country nearly a year working for a construction company that recently came into the limelight for all the wrong reasons- 'mistreatment of their employees, forced work without pay, unsafe worksites and more such inhuman atrocities'. "Why didn't he cut his losses and leave?" queried Ameena fighting back her tears. "The company held their passports so they couldn't leave", answered Jen, matching her friend's emotions. "That's illegal!", exclaimed Ameena. "Yes, but they don't know that. These people are flown in from rural, impoverished places and the company then demands they pay off the cost of their flight, accommodation and food. At the end of the day, they are paid next to nothing for overextended hours of work." Jen went on to explain. "It's all over the news. An undercover journalist discovered the appalling work conditions. His articles reveal the uninhabitable spaces they are given to stay where 8 or more people are crammed into one room with one common bathroom for the whole floor of such 'hostel dorms' as they were termed. The food was a gruel made of indetermined ingredients, unhealthy and unhygienic. And…" Jen paused in her discourse upon hearing the uncontrolled sobs that sounded in response. Ameena couldn't take any more. After a few moments of silence broken by sobs and sniffles, Ameena asked "Jen.. is he... did he make it?" and she was relieved beyond measure in receiving an affirmative 'uh-huh' in response. The mood changed and once again it was time for action. "Jen, you think we might be able to go visit him....uh where is he?". Neither of them knew the answers but they knew someone who would, the ever-resourceful Faisal.

It took a few days but Faisal who knew someone in the security who knew someone in the medical team found out all they needed to know. Meanwhile, the girls met with a couple of expat protection advocates who were already appraised of the incident. Soon the quintet was headed to the main hospital about 45 minutes away from the city centre where most of the airport staff lived in company subsidized condos. Faisal was given the name of one of the doctors in the ER who met them at the hospital entrance and led them to Malek's room. He was in post ICU care. The doctor checked on him before allowing the visitors of whom only two were allowed to go into the room. Ameena and one of the advocates representing the team, met with Malek and the doctor who shed more light on the matter.

As it turned out, after nearly a year of working with little to no salary, the company suddenly fired all the expatriate workers as soon as their illegal workplace practices were exposed. When the workers asked for financial compensation, they were refused and threatened with the risk of being deported and blacklisted from travelling back to this country. As the doctor helped translate Malek's words and tears, the story of the incident slowly and sadly unfolded. Malek had borrowed money from family members and friends to come to this country. The plan was to pay them back in installments from his salary. The dream was to build a big house in his village, buy back his wife's jewellery which had been pawned years ago and to save enough money to send his sons to the school in the city. When he ended up with no money, no prospects of another job and the threat of being blacklisted from travelling, he had lost all hope. He couldn't face the idea of going back home. In fact, he had no home to go back, he had borrowed against the house. So overcome with anxiety, he decided that if he was going to return home, he might as well return to a more eternal one. That way, perhaps the creditors may take pity on his family and forgive his debt or so he hoped, his final flicker of hope. At this point, his words gave way to a heavy substantial silence and their interview came to a sudden halt. It was the cue everyone needed to spring into action. Ameena and the advocate murmured some words of encouragement which seemed to have been lost in translation by the time they reached Malek and left the room. A few minutes later, the doctor joined the group of friends huddled outside the room, whispering loudly and animatedly. "This is a sad business. When my friend said that you were human rights advocates for expatriates, I hoped you could do something for him. Well, now that you have heard his story, what do you think?", asked the doctor. The animated voices lost their veil of whispering and everyone was concurrently offering ideas and action plans until no one could be heard clearly but everyone was heard too loudly for the hospital corridor. Reproaching looks from other medical staff quickly brought that to a halt and assuring the doctor of taking supportive legal action for Malek and others in his position, the quintet left the hospital.

Three weeks later a committee was officially commissioned to support expatriate workers. Ameena, Jen & Faisal joined the committee and set up a temporary shelter for workers who found themselves in financially dire situations. Four weeks later Malek was discharged and was brought to this shelter. Since then, laws have been created and implemented to protect the rights of expatriate workers, however, fraudulent practices still exist and the fight for justice continues.

*"the 'truth', however scary, holds healing in its wings.
A lie, however winsome, is kin to treachery."*

-asha (hope)

Yes, but...

He travelled often. She worked at the airport. His travels often transited through this airport. Her shifts overlapped with his travels. He liked to flirt. She liked the attention. He pushed the boundaries. She drew them, erased them and drew them again just as she pleased. It was a game. It was fun, for the most part anyway. It was sweet, until it became bitter.

Sheila had the kind of eyes that mesmerised, the kind of smile that captivated and a lilt in her voice that kept one hooked on her every word. Her words were well used too, intelligent, interesting, with a hint of invitation, just enough to leave the listener intrigued and wanting more. Alam was mesmerised, captivated, interested and intrigued. All the boxes were checked.

It began innocuously enough with a few greetings spoken while he waited for his connecting flight. As a consultant, he was highly sought after by many of the larger companies. With increased success, came increased travel. Sheila knew a lot about his life, his job, his clients, even some confidential things about them. He liked to talk. She listened, at least as much as she could while at work. Somewhere along the way, his transits spanned a day or a couple of days in the country. He invited her for coffee, she accepted. He invited her for dinner, she went. Dinners turned into breakfasts in his hotel room which became a sort of monthly ritual. A friend once asked Sheila, "So are you guys serious?" to which she replied with some old, frayed joke about people who are serious needing doctors. The friend did not laugh. Sheila did not explain the joke or her 'relationship'. They were just two people whom life kept bringing together and they accepted this happy intervention of fate without assigning much thought or consideration to it. They were whatever they were, and it was whatever it was.

Sheila wanted to become a registered nurse. The airport job was a way to save up money for nursing school. She had always been passionate about getting into the medical profession and at one point considered being a doctor but it was awfully expensive. While nursing school didn't come cheap, it seemed a more attainable goal. Alam was impressed and very supportive. While she was assiduous in her financial planning, the cost of supporting an ailing mother and a younger brother who was still in school didn't leave much in terms of savings for her. At the end of every month, her salary was deposited and, in a week, or two, it seemed to have all but vanished. Her brother went to a private school. He was just as ambitious as his sister, if not more and wanted to become a doctor. In the ninth grade, he was already studying for medical school entrance exams. She was proud of her little brother and ever since their mother became ill, she had taken over his care.

Alam was in awe of Sheila as she coped with all her many responsibilities. One night, as she lay in his arms, he said, "I don't know how you do it all. You work so hard and at such a young age. I've never heard you complain, not once." She just sighed and nuzzled closer. Sleep came easily. The next morning as they were getting ready to go their separate ways, he said with great deliberation, "You know, I hate for you to be in this situation. Working long hours and never being able to save enough. I wish there was something I could do to help." She was taken aback although not unpleasantly. Over the last few visits, their conversations had taken on a far more personal shape than the initial flirtatious ones. Yes, they had gotten very close thought Sheila to herself. She often did that, have private conversations in her mind. He responded to her unbeguiling stare with compassion and just a little bit of uncertainty. "Have I offended you? I didn't mean to. I truly want to help. I mean, we are…well we are…very close or at least I think we are…we have become…I just want to help", his words stumbled over each other just as unsure as the voice that produced them. "I am not offering you money or anything like that. It's just a bit of support, you know. You deserve it. You can pay me back when you start working as a nurse. Please say something." Her silence though not disagreeable was slightly unnerving. He was dressed and packed, ready for his flight back home. The taxi had been prearranged for 8 am. It was now 7.45 am. She was draped in a bedsheet, sipping tea and staring out of the window. She sat silent, not because she was upset but because she did not know what to say. She was grateful and embarrassed all at once. A little more of one and a little less of the other but which was which, she did not know. The next 15 minutes brought about a change in their relationship, a change in their lives that was unexpected. Between her silence and his compassionate persuasion, it was agreed that he would supplement her cost of living. Sealed with a kiss, the agreement hung in her mind like the grateful tears hung on her lashes. His phone notified him that the taxi had arrived. They kissed once more, and he left with a promise to see her again the following month.

Check out wasn't till noon, so she stayed in bed a little longer. As soon as he had left, a thousand words came to her. 'Thank you' being the most oft featured. It occurred to her that she hadn't even thanked him. Nods and tears were her entire contribution to the conversation that transpired between them. She was grateful, very grateful indeed. Yet there was something that sat uncomfortably in her mind like a pesky pebble in one's shoe. Now she felt guilty for feeling uncomfortable. "Oh, why is everything always so complicated with me. Here is a man who lov..umm.. cares for me and wants to help me. Why can't I just leave it at that? Even in my thoughts, I have to spoil a good time", and so went yet another private conversation in her mind. It was her day off. With no place to rush to, she and her unvoiced conversations drifted into an unsettled nap till it was almost time to check out.

Brunch with Lanya was comforting. Their conversations were light and filled with gossip. Which new staff member was shacking up with which old duty manager and who is getting promoted to senior beauty advisor based on qualifications not usually mentioned in a resume. Mimosas mixed with morsels of workplace mischief had the intended outcome of a good enjoyable afternoon. The bill arrived and Sheila was feeling generous. She insisted that it was her treat and paid for the both of them. Lanya looked at her friend who was usually very cautious with her expenses and understandably so, considering the numerous responsibilities on her slim shoulders. "Sheila, is there something you are not telling me?", she queried with a slight giggle which emanated partly from her sweet but impish nature and partly from the lavish servings of mimosas she had imbibed. "Why..whatever do you mean?" replied Sheila without answering the question. Lanya insisted. Sheila resisted. It was time to go home. They shared a taxi and Lanya who was not ready to give up just yet invited Sheila over to her place for a girls' day in. The warmth of the sun on her skin and that of the alcohol in her system made everything sound so amiable. She said yes. For the first time in months, perhaps years, Sheila felt unstressed. She was not worried about her mother's hospital expenses, her brother's school fees, her savings that refused to increase. She was not elated but she was not anxious, and it showed on her face, in her gait, in her uninhibited laughter. Lanya was curious and she would find the reason, even if it meant having to open that precious bottle of vintage champagne she had been saving for a special occasion. Her plan worked without fault.

Moments after they entered Lanya's little condo, Sheila found herself treated to champagne so smooth, sweet and bubbly, it could only be described as happy nectar. She felt like a care bear on a rainbow. She was drunk and out came the skeleton in the closet, body, clothes, trunk and all. Lanya was dizzy with happiness for her friend and also from the champagne but mostly with happiness. It was getting late, so the party was forced to end, and Sheila returned to her place. Both of them had early morning shifts the next day.

The next few weeks passed without incident. Lanya would occasionally tease Sheila about her "not-boyfriend-not-sugar-daddy-benefactor" and Sheila would retort in kind about Lanya's many (many) affairs. Alam would call every week and excitement began to build as the days grew closer to his next visit. During one of his calls, he gently mentioned that he had transferred some money to her account asking whether she had received it. She responded that she hadn't checked. After a pause, she said "thank you". It was abrupt and almost an exclamation, not at all how she had intended. A hesitant "you're welcome" came back. "Oh I don't mean to be so awkward about this Alam. I am grateful. I just..I don't know. I feel like this shouldn't be.. I mean, I know you are trying to help but...", Sheila tried to get the right words to explain her emotions but she couldn't. How could she when she barely even understood these emotions. All she knew was she felt a lot of them, or maybe they were just a few emotions in great quantities. "But what Sheila?", Alam's matter-of-fact question broke her train of thoughts. Once again, her words deserted her. Something about his soothing, persuasive speech always did that. It left her speechless. The phone call ended with news of his arriving on Tuesday and a quick "see you soon". Tuesday was only two sleeps away. That night she found it difficult to fall asleep. There was that pesky pebble in her thoughts again followed by something akin to guilt or embarrassment or some mutation of both.

His flight was on schedule. She had chosen the late shift so that it coincided with his arrival. As he exited, there she was waiting for him. Alam, tired as he was from work and travel, ran to her and took her in his arms. "Oh, how I have missed you!", he whispered in her ear. This was new, she thought. A happy new. A nice new. She smiled and her private conversation fed words into her voice, "I am happy to see you". Hand in hand, the happy couple walked to her car where one pair of hands were driving the car while the other pair of hands happily strayed. Once home, the straying continued all night long.

In the morning, Alam announced that he was staying for a few days this time. He had business in town. At his suggestion, she took leave for the next couple of days. They were going to get to spend a lot more time together. The next few days were a whirlwind of activities. The mornings were enjoyed on the beach and in the evenings, Alam took her to some of the most expensive restaurants and treated her like a princess. He even bought her jewellery. There was no mistaking where this 'not-quite-relationship' was going. If her friend had asked her the same question now about whether they were 'serious' Sheila would not joke in response. She would have answered with a firm and pronounced 'yes'.

Alam's business concluded; it was time for him to go back. The duration of her leave expired, it was time for her to return to work. Their love life seemed to be as transitory as his work life. "Each time I have to go, leaving you behind becomes more and more difficult.", Alam said as he was packing. She ran up to him and hugged him. It was a tight 'don't-let-me-go' embrace to which he responded in kind. "Why don't you come with me?" he said more than asked. Happy but surprised, once again she was speechless. When she finally found her words buried somewhere in her mouth, all she could muster was, "What..now?". He, however, seemed to come alive with the idea. He was beaming. "Yes, now. Why not? I mean who are we fooling? We obviously love each other so why waste time apart from each other?". "But what about my job?", she questioned unconvincingly. Alam sat her down and took her hand in his. Alternately kissing her hand and her face, he convinced her to apply for extended leave and travel with him for a couple of weeks. He would take care of everything. She could focus on her studies and apply to different schools if she didn't have to spend so much time working. He was helping her towards her goals. It was an all-round win-win situation. It sounded so good, she radiated his enthusiasm. It sounded too good, her enthusiasm dampened a little.

Sheila applied for emergency leave which was the only option at such short notice. Lanya heard about it at work and texted her. Sheila couldn't give too many details, mostly because she did not know much more than the fact that they were going away for a couple of weeks. Besides, Alam had asked her to keep their trip together a secret as they were entering the next phase of their relationship and he didn't want other people interfering and potentially ruining things for them. He wanted this trip to be all about him and her.

She hesitantly texted Lanya that she would be out of the country for a couple of weeks and she'd tell her all about it when she got back. "Out where?", Lanya demanded to know. It was not like Sheila to be so secretive. Relenting, Sheila replied "Turkey" and that was the last text that Lanya received from her.

Two days later, Alam & Sheila were on their way to enjoy their first vacation together. She was overjoyed. While at the airport, they stayed clear of the duty-free shops and Sheila's colleagues. She was a little less joyous. The boarding call started and Alam led her to the first class travellers lane. Her joy returned with gusto. Alam had bought the tickets, booked the hotels, managed the itinerary and paid for everything. This was a dream come true. She dreamt more, of quitting her job, of perhaps even attending nursing school in Europe. After all, Alam had clients and connections in many countries. Her dreams and their conversations took up the course of the flight. Soon they had landed, been transported by a cab waiting for them to the Palace hotel. The lobby looked like it was a still from the movie, 'Midnight at the Pera Palace', the only Turkish film Sheila had ever watched. Everything was rich and ornate. "So this is what luxury feels like", she thought, yet another private conversation starting in her head.

Upstairs, in their presidential suite, she began to unpack when Alam announced that he had a business meeting to attend. "But I thought, we were going to visit the local markets today", Sheila sounded a little disappointed although she found it difficult to be disappointed surrounded by such opulence. "Yes honey, we will. The whole day is ahead of us. I will be back soon, I promise. Why don't you rest for a bit? It's been a long journey", and with a quick kiss, he left for his meeting. The room had a grand balcony, the birds were chirping, the breeze was swaying the curtains and everything spelled relaxation in large drowsy yawns. She was smiling as she her head hit the down filled pillows. Ah, sweet slumber.

She heard her name as though in the distance. Opening her eyes slowly, still smiling, she scanned the room for Alam. "How did your meeting go?", she asked. "She's coming round", said a voice she did not recognize. "Yes, the poor girl is tired and I have kept her well supplied with champagne", said a voice that sounded like Alam's but surely those words could not be his. Two male voices laughed, a sneaky, greasy laughter. She closed her eyes again, hoping this was a dream, a bad dream. With a sinking sensation she realized it wasn't. The events of the past few days ran through her head at a dizzying speed. Alam had not let her get involved in any of vacation planning. She had no clue which street the hotel was on. There were no brochures, notepads, not even the menu inside the room with the hotel address on it. Unable to think clearly, she kept her eyes closed and pretended to be asleep while slowly reaching for her phone which she had kept near her pillow. She always kept her phone near her pillow. It wasn't there! She must still be drowsy, she thought. There must be some sort of explanation. Surely, there must be and with that conviction, she sat up and looked around the room, trying to appear calm. Alam was standing by the little kitchenette, a beer in one hand and her phone in the other while a stranger stood next to her bed in a state of half undress. Her calm appearance flew out the window, panic replaced it like a hurricane as her head drowned with weight of a fearful realization. "Alam, what is going on?", her words enquired but her tears pleaded against what she knew was going on. "Don't worry darling, it will be our little secret. No one has to know. After all, I am going to help put you through nursing school. Think of this as a little favour in return.", Alam's words slithered towards her unbelieving ears. "You do want to go to nursing school in Europe, don't you Sheila darling?" "Yes but,...". "You did say, you want to repay me for helping you, didn't you?". Gripped with fear, she muttered, "Yes, but..". Before she could finish, Alam interrupted her saying, "I have been very nice to you, haven't I? Buying you all those expensive gifts, bringing you on this all expense paid holiday, huh?". Sheila cried desperately "Yes, but I..". "Shhh...shh.. there's nothing to cry about. This is a simple business deal. That's all. He will spend an hour with you and then we will get to our vacation. He is an important client of mine. Now we don't want to displease him, do we?". She could only cry louder in response. Then nodding to the other man, he said, "I'll be back in an hour. Be gentle, won't you? She has to return to work soon and we don't want any bruises". "Gentle is my middle name", he sneered back, now sitting on the bed fully undressed. Shock, fear, disgust and disillusionment all mixed in a desperate concoction running through Sheila. She wanted to fight, she wanted to flee but all she did was freeze. Alam, his back turned, was at the door. The other man, a sweaty, lust blown letch of a creature was breathing on her face, his breath stinking of stale meat marinated in nicotine. She shrank back and shifted herself to the other edge of the bed until there was no where else to go. He caught her and pulled her towards him as she heard the door click shut at Alam's exit. Whether it was the man's slimy touch or the complete cognizance of 'betrayal', she suddenly unfroze! She kicked and screamed. She fought with all her might. The man, a little taken aback ordered her not to play hard to get. He had not paid for this kind of trouble. At the mention of 'payment', Sheila who had managed to get off the bed and run towards the balcony, felt nauseous. Her knees buckled and she fell to the ground. "Now that's better," grunted the man as he grabbed her once again. With one last effort to free herself, she bit him. She bit him hard and sank her teeth into his hand. This time, it was his turn to scream. Suddenly, the door flung open and the floor manager came rushing in with two of the housekeeping staff.

Sheila had an obsession with freshly laundered towels. It was one of her quirks. Even though she knew that the towels in her room were clean, she had called housekeeping and asked for freshly laundered towels to be delivered before falling asleep. When the housekeeping staff arrived, he heard screaming and yelling. He immediately notified the floor manager who rushed to the room. Their knocks went unheard by Sheila and her attacker in all the commotion. Once inside, the manager alerted the police. In a matter of minutes, the room was a flurry of activity. Sheila was slumped on the floor barely aware of all that was going on around her. She felt herself being carried and the next thing she knew was that she was inside an ambulance; thatshe was safe. A policewoman got into the ambulance with her. The last thing Sheila saw before passing out was the policewoman holding a passport, her passport.

"Hey there", murmured a soft, comforting voice as Sheila came to, from a drug induced sleep. Lanya was sitting by her side, holding her hand. She asked for water and sipping it, she took in her surroundings. "What happened? Why am I in a hospital?", Sheila wanted to know. Physically rested but mentally weary, she could not quite recall the events that led her there. Lanya helped her through the next few days as the police arranged for their travel back home and she also filled Sheila in with the missing parts of the story. After Sheila was rescued, they contacted her employer registered on the work visa stamped in her passport. Eventually, Lanya who was her 'emergency contact' and best friend was dispatched to bring Sheila back home. The rest of the information was supplied by the police. The man who attacked Sheila had been arrested but Alam or the man she knew as Alam had escaped. He is a little-known trafficker, and this was his first criminal activity in Turkey. There was an all ports warning out on him and the police were hopeful that they would catch him before long.

Relief at being rescued, stunned at being betrayed, Sheila said very little on their return flight. Once back home, she resigned from her job at the airport and moved in with Lanya. She needed time to think, time to heal, if healing was possible.

"an old mirror stood in the corner, pierced with shattered pieces of life, floating in the mirage of a silver lining."

-asha (hope)

An odd day...

She counted her steps. It had to be an even number. From the entrance to head office it was 92 steps, from head office to the purchase section, it was 46 steps and from there to the duty-free magazine section, it was 112 steps. However, if she was walking to a room with water like the kitchen or the bathroom or even to a place like the beach or the pool, then an odd number was tolerable because of the water. Did it make sense? No. Well, at least not to anyone else. As for what went through her head, no one else really understood.

Shafa had recently been recruited as an assistant purchasing officer at the new duty-free office. Shimmering with its tall glass windows that substituted for walls, the new office building stood proud in the heart of the city. The statement, 'it takes all kinds to make the world' was never truer than inside that building which hosted approximately 50 different offices. Every activity had its own department. Every department, its own head of department and consequent office. Then there were meeting rooms, huddle rooms which were just smaller meeting rooms and common rooms where people met but did not hold meetings. Shafa did not go very often to any of these rooms. She usually worked through lunch. The purchase department was busy year-round so there wasn't much time for lunch breaks anyway.

There was a big celebration in one of the common rooms and everyone was invited. Jess Janson had been appointed as the head of duty-free operations a year ago to the day and of course everything about Jess had to be celebrated. The staff acquiesced much as one does under a dictatroial rule. After lunch, as people started making their way to the party, someone passing Shafa's desk knocked over her coffee by accident. The coffee spilled on the price sheet she had been working on and it was ruined. This was not a good start to an event about which she already had a premonition. "Oops, sorry my bad", said Katie as she stopped to help Shafa clean up the mess. "It's ok. It's not you, it's just that kind of a day. It's not a good one.", whispered Shafa gravely. "What? Oh, yes of course, it's Monday.", joked Katie and ran off quickly to catch up with her friends. Once out of earshot she said to the others, "Well that was weird. I mean it's just coffee and her cup was precariously poised close to the edge of her table". "Oh, don't take any notice of what she says.

She has some sort of a condition", said one. "They say she has to take medication for it", joined another. "Yes, or else...", said Liam and mockingly growled at Katie. "Stop it. That's not funny.", scolded Katie who was sympathetic even though she didn't quite understand Shafa or her 'condition'. "Sorry. Anyway, we have got bigger problems to worry about", replied Liam, throwing his 'sorry' in the air while not quite apologising for his remark. "Ms. Janson is in another one of her moods", he continued. The group let out a collective groan.

Jess Janson was kind of like Miranda Priestly from 'Devil wears Prada' but without the good looks, the class, the style or the lovely twins. It was also suspected that she could not produce tears. It was once believed that she would not bleed if wounded but then she broke a tooth biting into a caramel apple and the red stream that gushed from her screaming mouth put an end to that rumour. They deemed her to be this worldly after all, at least partially.

Nobody wanted to celebrate Jess or Ms. Janson as she preferred to be addressed. However, it wasn't a matter of choice. When it came to the duty-free operations, Ms. Janson was lord and mistress of it all. If she says jump, you'd better not be standing on a balcony. You couldn't be seated if she was standing. Women were not allowed at work without makeup and caramel apples were banned in the building. Such was her reign of terror and none were more terrified of her than poor little Shafa.

It was 101 steps to this common room. "Uh oh!" thought Shafa. Then correcting this cosmic mockery by stepping in the same spot twice she entered the room, curbing her anxiety for the sixteenth time since

7 am that day. "Not good day. Today's not a good day and it's not because it's a Monday. That never has to anything to do with the kind of day it turns out to be. What silly ideas some people have!" muttered Shafa more audibly than she realized. Initially this quirk of hers was a little disconcerting to others, but she had been there for about four months now and everyone was used to find her muttering to herself. They paid no attention except for the likes of Liam who found it rather amusing and Ms. Janson who found it annoying. She never missed an opportunity to take a shot at Shafa. "Welcome Shafa, glad you made it. And there have been no calamitous oddities that crossed your path today I hope!", Janson said through a cackle, masking her jab as a joke. "Oddities.. get it?" Liam whispered to Katie, who sat unsmiling, thoroughly unamused by her boss and her colleague. Shafa stood silent close to the door as if ensuring her escape route should she need one.

"Where's Ed?" demanded Janson. Ed was the deputy head-of-department and her right-hand man. She relied heavily on his support at work. Office gossip had it that she relied much more heavily on him outside of work. It made perfect sense that they would be attracted to each other, after all they were two of a kind, a perfect match, a match made in hell, their homeland. Ed was a letch. The kind of pervert whose mere presence would corrupt the environment. When he entered the building, women intuitively felt a sense of approaching danger and fled for safety. All except Janson that is, she enjoyed his 'company' or so she was often heard to proclaim.

Katie nearly threw up at the mention of Ed's name. Even Liam seemed disgusted and that is saying something. Liam was one of those people who found everything amusing at everyone's expense. He wasn't odious in himself but it was difficult to get him upset about anything or even care about anything. It seemed like everything was fair game to him. Once he had witnessed Janson throwing a file full of important papers at Shafa hitting her in the face, narrowly missing her eye, with complete apathy. There were one or two other people about who went up to Shafa and ensured that she was alright. One of them brought her a glass of water. Of course, no one stood up to the boss from hell out of fear but at least the others showed some compassion towards her victim. Instead of drinking the water, Shafa dipped a paper towel in the glass and wiped the file whispering something about cleansing it. At that point her colleagues went back to their seats and Liam chuckled. Later he recounted this incident to Katie with Shafa's cleansing of the file as the highlight and laughed. "Something is not quite right with you, you know", Katie admonished him and walked away in a huff. He called after her saying, "but I didn't do anything". That was his level of detachment to anything and everyone. So, the fact that Ed disgusted Liam was saying more of Ed's ability to be nauseating rather than Liam's ability to commiserate. "He had called to say he'd be a little late", answered someone in the crowd. "Oh well, let's start then. I'll save him a piece of the cake.", said Janson slightly dampened in her enthusiasm. Anyone else could have been described as being disheartened but descriptors of heartfelt emotions normal to the humankind seemed essentially antonymic to her. "You'll give him more than that, wink-wink", murmured Liam with all the tact of a fruit fly on a hot summer's day. "Oh, shove off", snapped Katie who tried to find another place to sit, away from Liam. Thankfully, the party got going, taking away Liam's chance to respond. Janson cut the cake and some managers oozing with insincere paeans discharged their oleaginous words. Everybody else hurrahed, with all the joy people under the threat of dismissal for not joining in, can possibly hurrah. As cake was being passed around on very breakable plates for Janson would have nothing to do with inexpensive disposable plates, there came a hiss from the doorway, "forget the cake, I've brought the real party goodies.... hello ladies". Ed had arrived! His words making the ladies' skin crawl. He walked up to Janson and hugged her. While there was nothing one could point out as inappropriate office behaviour, a feeling of something lewd and vile disrupted the air as soon as those two touched each other. The hug prolonged and everyone averted their eyes. Katie, who loved cake, felt it turn rancid in her mouth. Giggling like a teenager, Janson unwillingly extricated herself from Ed's arms though not completely. He still had one arm around her waist or her shoulder..well it kept moving around her and she didn't seem to mind. "You brought champagne? At work?", piped Janson in a highly affected girlish voice looking at the bottle Ed had placed on the table. "oh don't worry, it's non alcoholic.", he replied. Then turning to the staff, he said, "besides I'm saving the good stuff for the after party at my place. Everyone's invited." Perhaps he imagined himself as someone loved by all, or at least someone not despised by all. Perhaps, he had expected a cheer of grateful acceptance from the onlookers. Whatever, he expected, all he got were a few obsequious yay's from the same managers who had praised Janson a few minutes earlier. Disappointed with this group who couldn't appreciate the magnanimity of his offer, he huffed, let go of Janson and picked up a plate, piercing the cake with far too much force.

"That is the 19th plate", counted Shafa desperately hoping for someone to pick up one more to even it out. Ed saw Shafa staring in his direction and mistook that as a cue. Walking over to her, his sleaziness spoke, "That loose jacket isn't hiding anything you know. Perhaps I can take you shopping some day, what say you?". Shafa panicked, stiffened. Filled with consternation her eyes darted around the room seeking help but no help came. Everyone was busy chattering over their pieces of cake. Janson's evil senses, however, smelled fear across the room and darted over. She saw Ed drooling over Shafa and rage infected her like yeast and she itched to put Shafa in her place. "Well well well, aren't we a sly one, huh, Ms. Shafa? Playing all naïve and coy...don't you know better than to flirt with your colleagues? This is highly unprofessional!", growled Janson at Shafa with unfounded accusations. "But.. but I.. I", stammered Shafa trying to explain something she didn't even understand. The room went silent. No one comprehended quite what had happened but one look at Ed standing next to Shafa and everyone guessed that this was a case of the age-old envy rearing its ugly head. Janson could not stand anyone else getting any attention, least of all from her man toy Ed. "I'll see to it that chief hears of this. Make not mistake you weird little fleabite, you are finished here!".

Ed wanted to slink away but noticed that people were gathering outside the room, curious at the ruckus. He tried to calm Janson down who was bellowing more than yelling. Shafa was on the verge of tears and Katie walked up to her with a glass of water when suddenly, Janson started to hyperventilate. Katie turned around and offered the water to Janson thinking she was just overexcited. "Water. Yes, water will calm you", advised Shafa, unthinkingly. That was the final straw. Janson lost her temper and hit Katie's hand which held the glass of water which flew in Ed's direction. Trying to avoid the glass, Ed tried to shield his face with his hands, the dessert fork still held in his right hand. The plate fell from his left hand on Janson's open toe-shod foot, the pain of which propelled her forward, stabbing her temple on Ed's pointed fork. She screamed and fell backwards hitting her head against the edge of the table. Down on the floor with a bleeding head and a smarting foot, she cursed everyone in sight and she did it loudly. The whole room now animated into a flurry of activity, people were scurrying back and forth, trying to get first aid for Janson. Katie called an ambulance. Everyone seemed to be doing something. Everyone except Shafa who was rooted to the floor, too afraid to move and Ed who was nowhere to be seen. That serpent had slunk away.

The ambulance arrived and after Janson was successfully abstracted from the premises, some of the staff stayed behind to clean up. The whole floor had heard of the afternoon's events and was abuzz with gossip which increased in intensity with every repetition. Somewhere on that floor someone heard that Ed had stabbed Janson in a valiant effort to protect Shafa. Unbelievable as it was, the serpent seemed to be turning into the saviour in this story. Reality still maintained a grip on some people like Katie who guided Shafa to the sick bay holding her all the way. Liam, bemused beyond words at how things unfolded, walked back to his office alone. Since he had no one to talk to, he counted the steps mimicking Shafa. It was all a joke, one big joke to him until his right foot reached the entrance to the office. 117 steps. He hesitated. "Don't be silly Liam", he chided himself. Then belying some deep-seated sense of self preservation, he stepped twice before entering.

The End

Notes:-

Notes:-

Notes:-

Notes:-

Manufactured by Amazon.ca
Acheson, AB

14075247R00049